2005

To John
"How Much
I Love You"

♡

Ellen

How Much I Love You

Written and Illustrated by
Felicia Rose Querido

Andrews McMeel
Publishing

Kansas City

How Much I Love You

02 03 04 05 06 WKT 10 9 8 7 6 5 4 3 2

ISBN: 0-7407-2717-6

Library of Congress Control Number: 2002102588

Book design by Holly Camerlinck

Attention: Schools and Businesses

Andrews McMeel books are available at quantity discounts with bulk purchase for educational, business, or sales promotional use. For information, please write to: Special Sales Department, Andrews McMeel Publishing, 4520 Main Street, Kansas City, Missouri 64111.

How Much
I Love You

One evening, as the sun set on an ant and his love, she turned to him and asked, "Do you love me?"

"Of course," he said.

"But I love you as the rivers love the rain, as the flowers love the sun, and the shore loves the ocean," she said and waited for his reply.

The ant was quiet. He didn't know
how the rivers loved the rain, why the
flowers loved the sun, or the
shore the ocean.

Long after his love went home, her words echoed in his thoughts, over and over, until the sun rose. Finally he said to himself, I must find out.

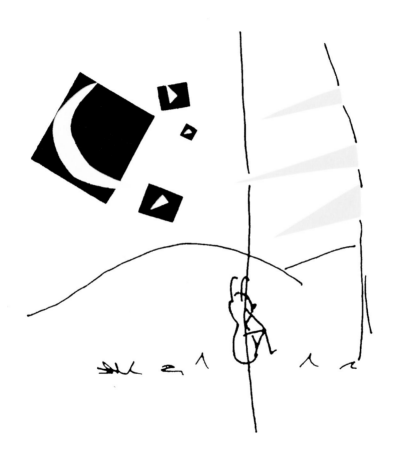

So he stood up and walked to the river.

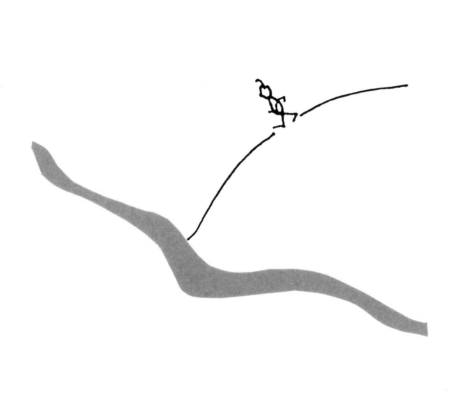

Climbing over the river's rocky banks,
he inched nearer the water. "Excuse me,"
the ant said over the river's gurgling,
"could you tell me why you love the rain?"

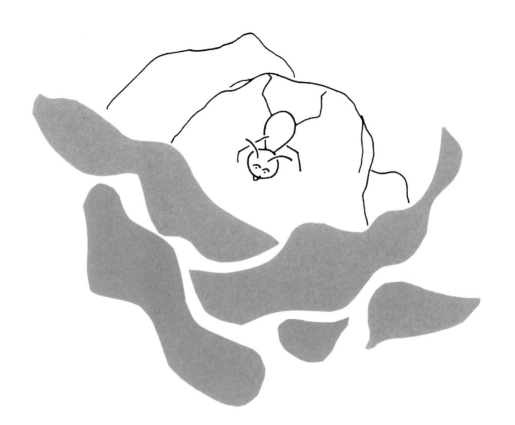

"Without the rain," the river sang, "my banks would dry up and I'd grow old. Every time it rains, I am renewed and get stronger. I could not exist but for the rain."

How can I keep my loved one young
when every year she and I grow older?
thought the ant. I don't understand.

And he knew he must talk to the flowers.

Down he walked to a field filled with wildflowers.

"Excuse me," he said to the flowers, "could you tell me why you love the sun so much?"

One very tall flower turned to the ant and said, "We love the sun because without it, we would not bloom. Our petals open only to be showered with its warmth. For this happiness, we will follow the sun wherever it goes."

This confused the ant. How could he help his loved one bloom without her having petals? I will have to keep asking, thought the ant. And he headed for the ocean.

*The ant walked through the night
to reach the ocean.*

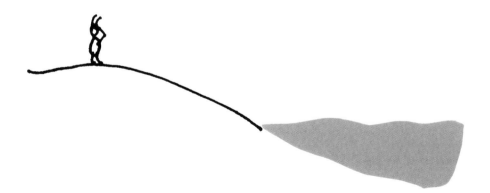

By morning, he could finally ask
the sandy shore, "Please, tell me how
you love the ocean?"

"All I can say," said the sand,
"is that I feel safe under its waves.
I love when it sweeps me away with it,
for when it leaves I am sad until it returns."

And the ant thought about
how much he missed his love.

As he walked home, he knew how the sandy shore felt. He wished he could feel his love's hand in his. As he drew closer to home, the sun was setting, and the ant looked for his love in their favorite spot.

Just seeing her alone made his heart race.

By her side, he took her hand, and asked,
"Do you know I love you?"

"Of course," she said.

"But," the ant said, "just as the ocean sweeps away the sand, I want you with me always. Like the sun shining on the flowers, it makes me happy that I can make you smile when you see me. Just as the rain seeks the river, my heart longs for you. You make me whole. I could not be who I am without you."

The ant grew quiet, and his love
said nothing. She squeezed his hand,
and they smiled and turned back
to the sunset.